Network
&
Multi-Level Marketing

Network
&
Multi-Level
marketing

By ALLEN CARMICHAEL

A revised 3rd edition

CONCEPT

By the same author:

"THE NETWORK MARKETING SELF-STARTER"
ISBN 1 873288 02 6
Concept - November 1991

"BELIEVE YOU CAN!"
ISBN 1 873288 03 4
Concept November 1992

"FOUR-SQUARE-SELLING"
ISBN 1 873288 04 2
Concept - Autumn 1994

The original edition of this book was titled **"MULTI-LEVEL MARKETING"**
ISBN 1 873288 00 X   *Concept* - July 1990
2nd Edition - retitled **"NETWORK & MULTI-LEVEL MARKETING"**
ISBN 1 873288 01 8   *Concept* - September 1991
Reprinted - June 1993
April 1994 (with additions)
Finnish language edition - September 1995

Book and cover design by Allen Carmichael
Printed in Finland by Werner Söderström Osakeyhtiö
Published by *CONCEPT* . PO Box 614 . Polegate . East Sussex . BN26 5SS . England
Telephone/Fax: 01323 485434

Introduction

You are about to explore one of the most effective and rewarding methods of marketing goods and services. It relies on a very simple basic principle - the concept upon which all of life is based - a family tree, the creation of one generation from another. In a word, *reproduction* or *replication.*

In the growth and development of a family, nature ensures that certain genetic information is handed on through the reproductive process from one generation to another, information that is essential to the family's successful survival and continuance. Exactly the same rules apply within the concept of a Multi-Level or Network Marketing organisation. For the constant expansion through successive levels or generations, the information needed to make the continuing development possible, is passed down the line from one generation to another.

It is just as important to understand what Multi-Level Marketing *is* as well as *what it is not.* Right from the outset of our investigation, let us be absolutely clear about two things:

MLM has nothing to do with *chain letters.*

MLM is *not* what used to be known as *Pyramid Selling.*

Multi-Level Marketing is an effective way by which either goods or services may be moved or distributed without the costs normally associated with a complex advertising, promotional and marketing operation. To the manufacturer it represents both cost-containment and a continuously increasing volume of sales, virtually dispensing with advertising costs and the need for a salaried sales force. It is, to the individuals involved in the MLM/Networking operation, a system of commission payments and incentives allowing each participant the scope and encouragement to build his or her own business organisation effectively so as to eventually achieve substantial rewards and, ultimately, if everything goes according to plan, complete financial independence.

The world is full of people seeking the easy way to riches and, unfortunately, MLM is sometimes presented in this get-rich-quick light. Nothing worthwhile ever came about without a struggle, and anything worthwhile has got to be worth striving for. People will talk of the glittering prizes, but that is not sufficient as an enticement to an intelligent person. What is essential in any situation where potential returns are high, is to know precisely what one must do to achieve these promised rewards. There must be a price to pay - life is charged by the minute! This book should give you the necessary key to open a door that literally can lead to riches - but only if it is approached with sound knowledge, and above all, the understanding of tried, tested and proven principles.

Network or Multi-Level Marketing is very much concerned with people, with the sharing of knowledge and with both *attitude* and *commitment*. What it is **not** is *Pyramid Selling,* as it used to be known. The so-called *Pyramid Selling* concept got a rather bad name some years ago and,

2

fortunately, parliamentary legislation was introduced which brought to an end practices that were quite unacceptable.

Multi-Level or Network Marketing has been in existence for 30 years. It is based on a pyramidal 'shape' for reasons that will become obvious as you explore further, but it is governed by strict controlling legislation (see *appendix 3*) which affords protection to both the individual and his rights. Furthermore, any company distributing its products through the medium of MLM has sound guidelines with which to comply both to the letter and the spirit of the law.

MLM is a system which bases its success on a very simple principle - a large number of people selling a relatively modest volume of the product. Everyone benefits and every individual has the same opportunity to go as far as his commitment and ability will allow. Napoleon once said, *'ability is of little account without opportunity.'* And it is exactly that - *opportunity* - that MLM offers. Some other wise soul once said that *'the opportunity of a lifetime should be taken during the lifetime of the opportunity.'*

Although relatively new to Britain and many other parts of the world, MLM is no stranger in the United States of America. Hardly surprising since that is the land of its birth. It has been well tried and tested and really does offer the opportunity of a lifetime, with one important proviso - the understanding that, to succeed, a lot of hard work is required. As with all things in life, if you embrace a project with the right degree of commitment and with the right attitude, you will surely not be disappointed. It is your personal efforts, not someone else's promises that will reap the rewards. If you enter a

MLM organisation with your eyes wide open and with this thought in mind, you have every chance of prospering.

As you must know by now MLM stands for Multi-Level Marketing. It could equally well stand for...

MEET - LEARN - MULTIPLY

as these three words adequately sum up the spirit of the concept.

A MLM company needs to seek out and **MEET** enthusiastic and ambitious people who wish to **LEARN** about its products and to understand the business opportunity being offered so that they, in turn, will go out and **MEET** others so that they, in their turn may **LEARN** and therefore **MULTIPLY**.

The company is simply relying on as many people as possible to go forth and spread the word as widely as possible.

And how should they best do this?

1. By meeting people, both friends and strangers and sharing the product with them. In MLM we do not talk of *selling* but of *sharing*.

2. By getting those who recognise the business opportunity to learn about the product and the marketing concept, then to go out and *meet* others who, in turn, they will teach, and by so doing...

3. ...*multiply,* thus increasing the constantly widening network of people.

MEET - LEARN - MULTIPLY

So, the company gives the individual the opportunity to build a *down-line* operation by *sponsoring* a number of *serious* and motivated people who will start the process of *reproducing* themselves by, in their turn, sponsoring their own equally committed individuals. Sponsoring in this way should be controlled - five or six people at a time is as many as most people would cope with. This process then continues down through several levels.

Earnings for the individual, which can be considerable, come from commissions and bonuses paid on the volume of product sold by each member of the network he or she brings into their organisation, plus of course, on the new members *those people* sponsor.

It is essential that anyone entering a MLM organisation really understands this concept if they are to maximise on the full potential of a modern and swiftly expanding industry.

This book is primarily intended as an introduction to an idea. It does not, and cannot, contain sufficient specific technical information to be regarded as in any way a comprehensive guide. All the MLM/Networking companies and organisations have their own systems and administrative procedures, but these are generally no more than minor deviations from the basic framework. It is that basic framework with which I am concerned - but with particular reference to the requirements any individual *must* understand so as to obtain the maximum benefits from a fascinating and highly rewarding experience.   Network Marketing has literally changed many people's lives. It is now active in all the major countries in the world.   You may wish to become a part of it - if you wish to prosper, the key to your success is simply to...

MEET - LEARN - MULTIPLY

Allen Carmichael - revised introduction, September 1995.
Original introduction to 'Multi-Level Marketing' - 1990
Revised - 1991 as 'Network & Multi-Level Marketing'
Reprinted June 1993 and April 1994

Chapter One

There are several recognised ways of distributing, and thereby selling, goods and services...

1. **Retail outlets** (see *Fig.1*)
   The small shop.
   The department store.
   The supermarket.
   They all stock goods - the public simply goes to buy.

2. **Direct selling** (see *Fig.2*)
   Usually this employs unsolicited approaches from a hopeful salesman seeking the opportunity to visit his potential customer with the aim of presenting his product or service.

3. **Tele-sales** (see *Fig.3*)
   Again an unsolicited attempt to sell goods or services over the telephone.

4. **Mail order selling** (see *Fig.4*)
   This is achieved either through advertising and the 'clipped coupon' response, or through the distribution of a catalogue.

5. **Multi-Level Marketing** (see *Fig.5*)
   This is often confused with *direct selling* but, as we can see, there are considerable differences.

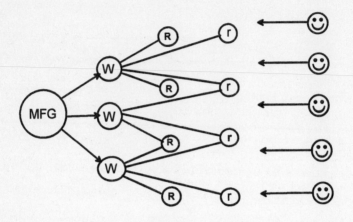

Fig.1   Manufacturer - Wholesaler - Large & small retailers

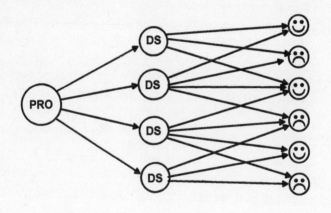

Fig. 2 Producer - Direct Salesman - Public

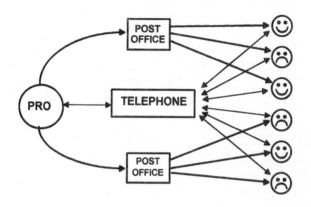

Fig. 3   Producer - Direct phone calls - Public

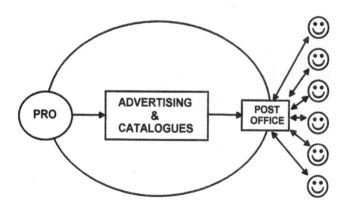

*Fig. 4 Producer - Advertising/Direct Mail/Catalogues -
Public*

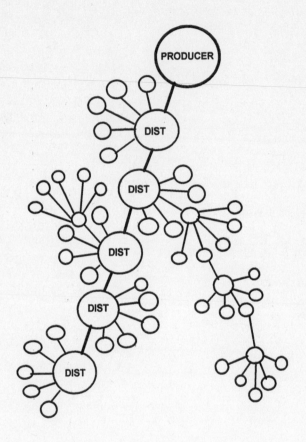

Fig. 5 Producer - Distributors - Distributors -
Distributors etc.etc...

Sales to the public at all levels - always at the same price.

A brief glance at the 5 diagrams will leave one in little doubt as to where the greatest benefits occur for sheer volume of distribution and greatest earnings to the largest number of people.

The real rewards in MLM come through *volume distribution* and the fact that each person sponsored has the opportunity to benefit, on that basis, from everyone he or she sponsors as his or her network grows and develops *down-line.* Sceptics may tell you you have to be in at the beginning to do well in Network Marketing. What they fail to realise is that *you are the beginning* of the down-line that starts with you!

At any level an individual may only want to be a *distributor*, and not be concerned with reproducing or replicating himself. This, of course, he can do, but he should understand that although he may do reasonably well with his small retail trade, he will not be exploiting the full potential offered within the expanding network he has joined. He or she will be missing out on the real rewards - those that lie in promoting the complete concept of multiplication. Remember, the clue to the real earnings is to...

MEET - LEARN - MULTIPLY

Sales should come simply as a natural outcome of the multiplication - the process of building your own organisation.

Look again for a moment at the illustrative diagrams for *direct selling* and *tele-sales* (*Figs 2 and 3* on pages 8 & 9). Notice the expressions on the faces of the customers! Many people do not appreciate - sometimes they even strongly resent - the 'hard sell' based largely on an attempt to influence a person who neither needs nor wants the product or service.

All selling is based on one simple word - *want*. Nobody, but nobody buys *anything* unless they *want* it. So, how does *want* actually come about? It is sometimes through the recognition of a *need*, or because something needs replacing through age or condition, but, more often than not, it is the result of either advertising, recommendation, demonstration or by having seen the product or been told about it by a friend, relative or neighbour.

A sale, at its very best, could be described as *letting the customer buy from you*. This is what is meant by *sharing*. In other words, the product or service speaks for itself, or better still, a third party has sung its praises so energetically that others have been influenced by their enthusiasm.

MLM does not demand *salespeople* in the accepted sense - for the concept does not call for selling in the accepted sense. The professional salesman - *'just show me the product and I'll shift it for you!'* - does not always do terribly well in Network Marketing, unless he is sufficiently flexible to see the way in which he will have to change his ideas and concepts. However, as you gain in experience, you will come to see that some networks place much more emphasis on selling than on recruiting or sponsoring.

Ideally, selling the product should come as the natural outcome of developing a network - and vice versa, for sales and down-line development are totally linked together. Obviously sales are important, for without them, nobody gets paid! There is no escaping that as a fundamental truth.

One of the most important ingredients for success is *belief.* Without belief in the MLM concept as a wealth-generating occupation, you would not get very far. But *belief* comes in a variety of forms:

1. **Self belief** - your belief in your own ability to become a success.
2. **Belief in the product** or service you are selling.
3. **Belief in MLM itself** as a concept offering rewards in direct ratio to your ability and commitment to *teach* others and thereby *multiply* - and the rewards can be very high indeed!

The yardstick then, is not how good you are at selling the product, but rather, how good you are at *selling the concept* and how good you are at *teaching others* - passing on what you have learned about MLM to the next level in your developing down-line.

If you have belief in your product, *use it yourself* then tell your friends about it - natural sales will certainly result. As we have said, the word in MLM is *sharing* not *selling*. And here you have a double-edged sword, for you have two things to share - the product and the *opportunity*.

Sharing is one of the most rewarding of human activities, and through sharing you are developing your network by *sponsoring* others, who, in their turn, will share and sponsor so that the product is always on the move and, like the roots and branches of a tree, the network is always growing and expanding.

Simple, isn't it?

But to grow and develop a large and successful business and benefit from the rewards that will bring, other human ingredients are needed. The most important of these are *attitude* and *commitment*.

Attitude embodies so many things, not least of which is *belief*. Attitude has to do with the way in which you both perceive and present yourself. Appearance, dress, the car you drive, but above all, the feeling you have about yourself and about what you are doing. It is to do with how you present the *opportunity* to the people you hope to sponsor. If your thoughts are dominated by the idea of bringing people into this business simply that you may benefit from their activity, believe me, you are on the route to failure! That would be an example of *attitude* working in precisely the wrong way. Your attitude must inspire total confidence and, most important of all, you must be credible to the people you hope to interest.

Do you see yourself as successful?

There is a saying that *'you are as you appear'*. If this is so it is important to present yourself as a successful person. People will accept you at the face value you place on yourself. Dress the part, play the role, and you will be the person you *feel* yourself to be!

Attitudes are so easily conveyed to others. We all unconsciously read the signs offered by body language, dress and presentation. We tend to make immediate judgements based on these visible manifestations of attitude. Never forget that others are basing their judgement of you on exactly the same things.

So, it is important that if we wish to have credibility, we must be sure we are presenting the right signals. These things cannot be contrived - there is no use in attempting to be something you are not. Shakespeare said it all - '...*this above all, to thine own self be true and, it must follow as the night the day, thou cans't not then be false to any man.'*

Since you only have one chance to make a first impression, be sure that you don't blow it!

If you are to instil confidence and teach others to do the same in the development of your network, your image and

14

attitude must be impeccable. You have a *responsibility* to pass on all you know if you are to prosper, so it is in your own interests to set the vital standards. If people believe in you they will willingly take you as a role model and emulate everything you do - and that means that they will be passing on the same feelings to the next generation in the network.

Sponsoring must be rooted in *belief.* It is important to believe in the person you are sponsoring since you are going to expend a lot of time and effort in teaching them to sponsor and, in turn, teach others. In any business, all attitudes emanate from the top. *You* are the top in your own organisation, and you set the standards on which your income and the income of others will depend. It is your responsibility to teach others about the product, how to order it, how to keep records and generally be business-like in organising themselves in the development of their own down-lines.

There is equal opportunity for everyone to travel as far down the MLM route as they wish - and as you must have gathered by now, it is a route that can lead to considerable rewards. It is quite feasible to achieve financial independence in just a few years! All that it takes is a real steadfastness of purpose. It really is as simple as A-B-C...

ATTITUDE...BELIEF...COMMITMENT

Chapter two

The product of a Network Marketing company is usually one of high quality.

It needs to be, to inspire the necessary degree of confidence and belief in those who are going to move it. As we have already seen, cost-containment is the big attraction to the producer or manufacturer, therefore he is usually prepared to expend more on research and product development, providing a product often of higher quality than its competitor's, being sold through the more conventional retail outlets. That is the ideal, but it has to be said, not *always* the actual case. Unfortunately there have been, and always will be, MLM operations in which the quality of the product falls short of the needs and ideals of the concept. The outcome is nearly always the same - *they fail, and occasionally*
bring the industry into disrepute.

By sharing the product with friends, family and acquaintances you may simply be replacing something they already have or use with a product your belief and attitude show them to be better. Sharing the product is all the 'selling' you are likely to do. The people you share with in this way may well turn out to be the people you choose to eventually sponsor. Always remember, though, sponsoring requires a high degree of commitment on your part. This cannot be stressed too strongly, for if you do not feel real commitment you could be doing that person a distinct disfavour - and by the same token, letting yourself down since that particular leg of your down-line would certainly stop there.

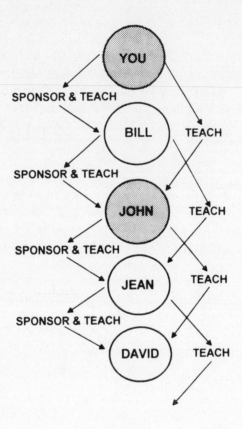

Fig. 6

Teach people to teach is the key to MLM - unless that happens - just like failing to water a plant - the growth ceases and the plant withers and dies. Nothing is secure until *you have reproduced yourself* - and that happens only when the *third level* is in place (see *Fig. 6*)

18

As I have already pointed out, the purpose of this book is to help you understand the concept of MLM and to give you an effective way of teaching those you sponsor. It is also aimed at helping you develop the correct attitudes to maximise on the potential of the business on the brink of which you stand right now. It is vital to the development of your down-lines that everyone is taught the same things and that everyone develops the same working habits and uses the same language.

You are bound to come up against objections - and this is the completely natural outcome of confronting anyone with a brand new idea or concept for the first time. Initial scepticism is to be expected. The most common objection is based on a misconception - Pyramid Selling - so let's get this out of the way right now.

MLM and Network Marketing are merely two names for the same concept. *Pyramid Selling* in the form that gave it such a bad name some years ago, *no longer exists.* Legislation has put a welcome stop to the unethical practices that gave this form of selling and distribution the bad name it earned (see *Appendix 3* at the end of the book for more information).

The concept was one of selling a product down-line with an ever-increasing price as it moved from distributor to distributor. At some point the product would out-price itself and become virtually unsaleable. Only those close to the top of the 'pyramid' could hope to gain the rewards the schemes promised. Further, there was usually no arrangement for the producer or manufacturer to buy back surplus stock, so people tended to get stuck with a lot of product they could not sell.

The system exploited both the seller and the buyer.

With MLM, *the wholesale price of the goods never alters*, no matter how large an organisation becomes. The high earnings that are possible through a good MLM company simply come about through *over-rides* paid on the volume of product moved by the developing network through successive generations. *Everyone* is at the top of their own network development. The individual has both an *up-line* and a *down-line*. Your *up-line*, being responsible for those he has introduced, benefits from what you are doing, whilst you benefit from the activity of the development *down-line* from you, for which *you* are responsible - the outcome of all your hard work, effort and support.

Anyone can be successful if he or she keeps in mind the simple A-B-C we have already discussed - and, just in case you may have forgotten, MLM stands for...

MEET - LEARN - MULTIPLY!

The sceptic - and there is always an abundant supply - may still point out that MLM seems to be based on a *pyramid.* Ask him if he knows anything about the usual corporate structure, or the structure of a charitable organisation, a political party or a religious order. Get him to tell you how many chairmen a large company has. The answer will be *one*. Jot down C on a piece of paper. Ask him how many directors, regional managers, group or departmental managers, and finally, how many employees there might be. As he answers, write down the results in the form of a pyramid - as in *Fig.7.*

The pyramid structure is the strongest organisational concept man has devised. Any Network Marketing organisation is bound to look like a pyramid, but that does not mean it has anything to do with the concept everyone remembers that was known as pyramid selling.

Fig. 7   Chairman - Directors - Managers - Employees

Chapter three

MLM is, as we have seen, based on the simplicity of multiplication. In explaining and demonstrating the concept to a prospective participant, you really cannot be too simple in the way you make your presentation. Start by demonstrating the simple mathematical progression of doubling up...

$$1 \times 2 = \underline{2} \quad 2 \times 2 = \underline{4} \quad 2 \times 4 = \underline{8} \quad 2 \times 8 - \underline{16}$$

Adding all the underlined figures, the total = **31**

This might strike you as rather childish, not to say obvious, but the whole object of the exercise is to implant this simple mathematical progression in the mind of your prospective recruit right from the outset. The idea behind this exercise is to point out that if each person in a developing down-line *sponsors* and *teaches* only 2 other people, and the system is continued, the 'culture' grows at a surprising rate - and this is what sponsoring in MLM is all about.

Now to the next step. Supposing each person sponsored, not 2 people each, but 3, just look at how the total is affected...

$$1 \times 3 = \underline{3} \quad 3 \times 3 = \underline{9} \quad 3 \times 9 = \underline{27} \quad 3 \times 27 = \underline{81}$$

The total now amounts to **121**

Now let's jump a stage and assume that each person sponsors and teaches 5 others.   What happens to the multiplication under these circumstances is quite startling.

$$1 \times 5 = \underline{5} \quad 5 \times 5 = \underline{25} \quad 5 \times 25 = \underline{125} \quad 5 \times 125 = \underline{625}$$

The total now is **781**

The difference is a surprising 660 more than in our previous example!   The point to make here to your prospective recruit is that nobody should have any real difficulty in finding an initial *five* people to sponsor. If you were asking them to find and sponsor twenty five,   things would certainly be more difficult. But *five...!*

Human nature being the frail thing that it can be,   some people will become so excited by this presentation that they will want to leap ahead, because bringing in only five people seems to them so easy.   They want to start empire building as quickly as possible!   They see the answer as sponsoring as many people as possible, as quickly as possible *to make it all happen faster!*

DANGER!

Remembering what sponsoring implies and requires of the individual,   this idea *must be killed immediately.*   Your down-line people *must* realise that *total commitment to teaching newly sponsored people all you have taught them* is the absolute rule.   Any deviation from this,   through over-sponsoring, is a recipe for disaster.   If teaching and motivating is to be thorough, it is imperative to stick to only five or six new people at a time.

Suppose you were to sponsor 24 people and attempt to get each of them to sponsor 24 themselves, the scenario would be this:

1. You would have your 24 to teach, train and motivate.
2. In the third level of your down-line there would be 587 people to deal with - and it would be *your* responsibility to assist your initial 24 in teaching and supervising those people.

Perhaps now you can see the sense and validity of teaching restraint. If MLM is *really* going to work for you - as well as everyone else in the development - do not allow the people you sponsor to get things out of proportion, and by so doing, let the whole thing run out of control.

Sticking to five, for the sake of our example, let five become a magic number. That way things remain manageable with only 5 to teach and 25 to help with - and yet still, at the 5th level, you will have an organisation of 781 people *securely in place.* This way your earnings will grow steadily until they are very interesting indeed. At that ultimate stage you would probably be earning more in a month than many people earn in a year!

When a new building goes up, it starts with secure foundations, and all possible care is taken to ensure that everything has been done correctly, nothing has been left to chance, and nothing overlooked. The progress of the building seems amazingly slow at this stage of its development. That is because the success and stability of the eventual structure *depends entirely* on getting the foundations right.

It is exactly the same with a painting. If it is to last and survive, the painter knows that the very first application of anything he puts on his canvas *must be right* since everything else he lays on top of that will rely, for its stability and permanence, on the correctness of the priming or undercoat.

Just as with the building or the painting, if we aim to create a structure of permanence we must be sure the foundations are well laid. We are basing our structure on building levels of five or six people, but to *find* your five or six really *serious* people, you may easily have to sponsor as many as 15 to 20 before you have identified the *right* five. This is not contradicting what I have already said about numbers. So long as you are able to identify the five you are looking for, the extra numbers will very likely be people simply interested in making a bit of extra pocket money - and you will have acquired 15 *dealers* or *retailers*, people who will help keep the product moving. This is all business to you as you will be supplying them with the product(s) and benefiting from the sales they achieve, not to mention any bonus payments on volume sales from the whole of your down-line. But the people *essential* to your plan are the five or six *serious* ones.

Going back to the example of the high-rise building, it is surprising, once the foundations are properly laid, just how fast the structure rises. In fact the momentum appears to increase as each successive level is added. It is exactly the same with your MLM organisation - remember the multiplication?

You are going to be involved in two kinds of *prospecting...*

1. Prospecting for possible sales situations - but, more importantly

2. Prospecting for the people you need to sponsor to stimulate the growth of your business.

The word *prospecting,* to most people, conjures up pioneering and the search for gold. And that is precisely what it is! We are searching for gold. So the aim of prospecting must be to seek opportunities in the most intelligent way to maximise our chances of success. Remember...

YOU DON'T LOOK FOR GOLD
IN A COAL MINE!

(For more information on prospecting,
turn to *Appendix 1* at the end of the book)

Chapter four

In order to head off a few possible potential disasters, let's summarise what we have learned so far...

- MLM depends for its success and future on the constant development and expansion of a network.
- MLM is a highly effective way of marketing a product or service using the concept of a large number of people each moving a modest volume of the product.
- Your belief in the product is essential - you use it and you share it with others.
- Your initial aim is to sponsor 5 *serious* people.
- Your next task is to teach them, in turn, to find their own 5 serious people.

If you acquire a few *dealers* or *retailers* during the process of sponsorship, all to the good, as that way, the product is always kept moving and you will benefit from the sales they make.

Now let's dig a little deeper and look at further implications and examine a few of the notable pitfalls that most people encounter.

Recalling the mathematical progression...

1 - 5 - 25 - 125 - 625 - 781

If 781 people use the product themselves and have shared it on the 'modest amount' basis with friends and neighbours, a tremendous volume of product has been moved - and that is taking no account of the *dealers* and *retailers* that many people in the network will have in their down-lines.

PITFALL NUMBER ONE:
...to forget the magic number 5!

All of your future success is based on this, and *not* on over-extending and attempting to sponsor 25, 50 or 100 people in the misguided belief that you are speeding things up. This is like laying a shallow foundation to the high-rise building. *Strength lies in depth not in width!*

PITFALL NUMBER TWO:
To go out deliberately seeking salespeople. The salesman's natural instinct is to sell *as much* of the product as possible. You may feel there is nothing wrong with that, and that sales people are usually highly motivated individuals, and as such, are well worth sponsoring. They are certainly not afraid of a bit of hard work. However, they must modify their ideas somewhat if they are to achieve the high rewards that are possible in Network Marketing. They must understand that if all their efforts are to be put into *selling*, they will be placing restrictions on themselves, for they can only sell so much in any given time. If they understand that through *sponsoring* and getting other people to sell and sponsor, they will eventually benefit in a much more spectacular way, they will be on their way to seeing the real rewards.

The 'super-salesman' does everything to excess! In setting out to sell all he can, he is constantly seeking the recognition and approbation of his peers. If he can be persuaded, and he does latch onto the idea of sponsorship, the danger is that he may throw himself whole-heartedly into the fray because he suddenly sees himself as heading up a private sales force! In sponsoring more people than he could ever manage to teach and support properly, very soon everything begins to crumble. When he is sponsoring his 57th person, what is happening to numbers 1, 2 and 3? They have probably become totally demotivated through neglect, lost interest and have drifted away. The first floor of the building has gone up before the foundations have been properly laid and, quite frankly *it will not work!*

People very easily start to drift away if there is insufficient support and directional instruction. Eventually our super-star salesman gets discouraged himself and wanders off in search of the next product to sell. *End of story.*

THE PEOPLE YOU SPONSOR NEED ALL YOUR SUPPORT AND ENCOURAGEMENT - *CONSTANTLY!*

Some time ago, in the United States, a survey was carried out in an attempt to discover why the sales side of the Life Assurance industry has such a high turnover of people. 2000 people were interviewed, all of whom had 'failed'. The common denominator turned out to be *'nobody told me what to do!'* What a terrible indictment of an industry - and, sad to relate, much the same situation would probably have been revealed here.

Human beings are amazingly frail and vulnerable, constantly in need of both support and recognition. *Support* to give them directional guidance - what to do and how to do it - and *recognition* because that is *the single most important motivational factor to any human being.* Most people, if asked, would say that *money* is the most important motivational factor. They would be wrong! Of course, it is *money* if you don't have any, but once you have, *recognition* takes its place. (See *Appendix 2* at the end of the book)

PITFALL NUMBER THREE:

To believe that by sponsoring 5 serious people you have reproduced yourself. You have not done that until the *third level* is in place. Only at that stage are the foundations properly laid, and you could say you are truly duplicated.

To illustrate this, take as an example, your own sponsor. Supposing that, having brought you into the organisation - but before you had been taught sufficient to allow you to go out and start actively sponsoring your own people - *he had opted out!* Even before you had had the chance to see the benefits of MLM working. How would you feel? Let down? Abandoned? Disillusioned? You would almost certainly drop out as well. Your sponsor's credibility would be precisely *nil...* and probably so would the credibility of MLM.

If, on the other hand, your sponsor had helped you in every way he could, and you had your own first 5 people in place, benefiting from your knowledge and expertise, had he then opted out, it would not significantly have affected your situation or your future in the business.

So, to emphasise the point again...*you have not reproduced yourself until the third level is securely in place* (see *Fig.6* on page 18).

Once that all important third level is in place, things are really beginning to happen, and all the proof you should need to convince you of the viability of MLM is beginning to manifest itself.

Having established that third level (Jean in *Fig.6*), if you were to move away to devote your time to teaching others, this line of development would be secure - and providing Jean and John were people of the right calibre, that down-line would continue to expand and prosper. Everyone who has been successful in MLM - and there are very many - has done so because they fully understood this principle of reproduction or replication, *and acted on it.* This point cannot be emphasised too strongly.

No doubt your sponsor saw *you* as a person of high calibre. In seeking your 5 serious people it is most important that you only sponsor people that you see as at least your equal. You are not seeking out lesser mortals to fulfil the role of *employees.* You are looking for people you see as being *at least as good as you,* since your eventual success will depend on maintaining the *quality* of the individuals that join as your down-lines go deeper. The people to look for are *Gold Bricks!*

If we consider that eventual number we arrived at for our organisation - **781** - common sense must tell us that it is most unlikely we could maintain a 100% quality factor throughout the entire development. We are dealing with human beings, and standards are bound to slip here and there diluting the overall quality as the multiplication continues downwards and outwards. There are simply not sufficient *Gold Bricks* in the community to populate our Utopian situation!

As we know, your job is to *duplicate* yourself. Do not settle for anything less. If you can instil the importance of *the quality factor* into your line of 'generals' - the serious 5 - and make them realise how special *they* are, they in turn will seek out their own generals, not privates! As we know, in looking for generals, privates are bound to appear, but these will become your *dealers* and *retailers*.

I realise I am being very repetitive, but if I am to be instrumental in turning you *into the success you want to be,* I cannot emphasise the importance of certain key aspects of our plan too strongly. The strength in your line of sponsorship lies in maintaining the quality factor as well as sticking to the principle and concept of sponsoring, and teaching others to sponsor in fives or sixes.

Why do I emphasise this so strongly? Because five is the number that can most effectively be managed by one person. This has been proved in and adopted by both industry and the armed forces as the most viable principle of management.

This book is intended to lead you through the basics of MLM and to assist you to teach others. For the concept to work to the benefit of all those involved, the most ethical standards must be maintained. This cannot be a comprehensive training manual, and that certainly is not what was intended.

My aim is to produce the motivation necessary to fire *your* enthusiasm so that you, in your turn, can fire the enthusiasm of others.

MLM can benefit everyone and yet takes advantage of no one. Correctly taught and operated, the concept is capable of great wealth generation. It has significantly altered the lives of very many people throughout the world, bringing a quality and purpose where perhaps there was not much of either.

MLM feeds off commitment.   Those who stick to its simple philosophy and do not allow themselves to be constantly distracted by endless green-field opportunities are the ones that eventually prosper and enjoy all the benefits it can provide.

Chapter five

Any journey, no matter how long, starts with just one step.
That step is the commitment to start.
You have decided this is really what you want to do, and
realise that if you perform to the very best of your ability, you
could achieve financial independence in just a few short years.
Many people dream of early retirement, but very few ever
actually manage to make it a reality. You have arrived at a
point in your life where that dream is a distinct possibility!

That has got to be a very exciting realisation and should
supply all the motivational stimulation you need to begin the
journey. You must accept that in life there is always a price
to pay. Nothing is for nothing. To get started is going to
take effort and dedication. Supply those two ingredients and,
before very long, you will be coasting along quite easily.

Two colourful analogies come to mind...
In my childhood I lived not far from a canal and I was always
fascinated by the mighty Shire horses that were used in those
days to pull the heavily laden barges. The horse would strain
every muscle as its great hooves dug into the tow path, the
tow rope stretched to what seemed breaking point. Almost
imperceptibly the barge would begin to move, and quite
soon, the rope would droop towards the surface of the water
in an easy curve. From that moment on, all the horse had to
do was saunter along whilst the barge glided gently and easily
behind.

Have you ever pumped water up from a well? If you
have, and the well had not been used for some time, you will

know that long and sustained effort on the pump handle is needed to draw the water up to the surface. If you paused for a rest, the water would slowly sink back down the pipe until your efforts were resumed. Eventually water began to flow from the pipe, and to maintain that flow, only a very minimal effort was required on the handle.

So, take your choice - the canal horse, or the water pump! The message is the same - hard work and a committed effort until things start to move, and from then on, life begins to become easier.

SO...WHERE DO WE BEGIN?

1. *Don't be afraid to jump in with both feet!*
Be prepared for hard work and to make some sort of financial outlay. *Speculate to accumulate!* The amount of money you may be expected to outlay will vary from one MLM company to another, and will depend, to some extent on the nature and price of the product(s).

Regard this initial outlay as your *stake money* - a small investment with the greatest potential return of any money you have ever staked. You are investing in yourself, never forget that. The returns can be immense just so long as you do things correctly - and, I venture to suggest, with this book in your hands, you certainly could never say *'nobody told me what to do'*!

Too many people fail because they think they know best- they cannot resist trying for ever to reinvent the wheel. This book is telling you exactly where they went wrong, showing you what to avoid and what you must do to *guarantee* your own success - but only if you stick to the rules and to the tried and tested methods.

2. *Use the product - share the product!*

Your personal endorsement of the product will give others great confidence. It is your *credibility factor.* In using the product yourself you must believe in it, and quite naturally, you will be able to feel excited about it in talking to other people. Your excitement will very quickly convey itself to others.

3. *Keep pumping - get the system flowing!*

Remember, the water takes time to reach the surface, and comes out of the pump slowly at first. But soon you will have a veritable flow.

It is now time to start digging deeper and developing downwards...

5	It is now time to excite and stimulate others,
25	always keeping in view the aim of getting that
125	all-important 3rd level in place. It is only then
625	that the pump is really gushing - and the financial
781	rewards begin to appear.

4. *Keep sharing - keep teaching!*

Continue to share the product with your network, helping the people you have sponsored to find their own serious five. You can afford to develop the retail side of your own business now, as well. At this point there is no harm in taking on a few more part-time people in need of a secondary income .

5. *Yes!... Five!*

That all-important number appears yet again! But please, don't forget, flexibility is the name of the game. Some companies prefer to teach the concept of recruiting in, for example, *sixes.* This doesn't in any way alter the concept - all it means is that everything is based on a different multiple. Whatever number you operate with, *stick to it.* Be sure it is burnt across your brow in letters of fire! This is the key to control, and therefore *success.*

At this point it would be appropriate to look at ways of helping you to *prospect* for your initial five.

Prospecting is all about attitude and belief.

Your attitude will have an effect on the people you meet and it is your belief in the product and in the concept of MLM that will be your basic ingredients. Attitude is the natural outcome of both those beliefs. If you feel your product is splendid and you are personally excited by the business opportunity you are able to offer others, your natural enthusiasm cannot fail to come across and impress people.

Start by making a prospect list. You should aim to get down the names of at least 100 people. This is not as easy as it sounds, but if it is approached in a methodical way, it is not really so difficult.

Your list should contain people from every walk of life, ideally people who have had at least some degree of success in life. If they show something of the entrepreneurial spark, even better, for that is what is needed if the aim is eventual self-employment.

They should be people you can talk to easily. After seeing your enthusiasm, very few of them will turn down the suggestion that they should hear about an idea that could lead to substantial extra earnings and the enrichment of their lives. After all, you didn't!

Think of prospecting as simply *the sharing of an opportunity.* If you know of something that could alter the course of other people's lives, isn't it natural that you should want to share the good news?

There are people who might see what you have to tell them about MLM as an opportunity to exploit other people. If this is the case, believe me, *they will not succeed.* Don't encourage them and don't try to change their outlook, for their attitude will be detrimental to your own development.

It is a positive attitude of natural excitement and enthusiasm that will convey itself to others and convey interest and a wish to know more. If these are not attitudes you can recognise in yourself, it could be that *you* are not looking in the right direction yourself...

In drawing up your list, divide you life into a number of headings...

Who was I at school with?
Who do I work with?
Who do I play sport with?
Who do I know from a club, church, political party etc.?
Who do I know through my marriage?
Who do I know through my children?
Who do I buy goods and services from?
Who is the most successful person I know?
...and so on, and so on...

If you think along these lines, you will be surprised how many names you will actually come up with. Prospecting is no more than living in a community with your eyes and ears wide open. You could use a third party approach. Tell anyone you know that you have a fantastic business opportunity to offer anyone with a bit of drive, and ask them to tell you the most successful person they know. Now who could resist asking you what the opportunity is? And before you know it, you are explaining everything! Human nature is such that there are very few of us who could resist asking about something that is going to better our lives.

How many people would you say are really happy doing what they do for a living? If you were to ask the question *'do you see yourself doing that for the rest of your life?'* you would soon find out! And there is a great conversational opening. How many people would say *'no'* if you asked whether they could use some additional income? Would they be interested in hearing about a way they could earn extra money on a part-time basis? Or, do they know anyone to whom this idea might appeal...

Make your list as long as possible and try to add to it all the time. Carry it with you always as new people will keep cropping up in your mind. Don't try to remember them - *write it down straight away.* If you don't do this immediately, you will certainly have forgotten by the time you get home. Carry this book with you and use the pages provided at the back to maintain a good prospect list.

Look for people you see as having *credibility.* Think ahead to the next generation in your networking development. The people you are talking to are the ones who will eventually have to do what you are doing, and it is in your own best interests that they have the credibility to do it.

When you start to use your list, don't use up all your best prospects at first. You will find that, with experience, you will develop your own technique for speaking to people and making your presentation - and you will get better and better at it. Far more sensible to cut your teeth on people you don't know very well and save what you imagine to be your best prospects until you feel totally confident and more professional. Be prepared to lose a few prospects in the early stages until you have built up the necessary confidence. Be as conversant with this book as possible. If you like the diagrams, learn to use them yourself as a means of putting across the concept of MLM easily. If you feel the book has been of significant benefit to you, lend it to others as it may help to explain things to them better than you feel able. So, save your best prospects until you have the confidence and knowledge to be really credible and can put across your message as well as the person who influenced you.

You cannot hope to teach others about MLM until you have learned as much as possible yourself. Take time. This is your investment. Take care. You only get one chance to present the idea to a new prospect.

As we have seen, it is no bad thing to collect a few part-time dealers or retailers. Similarly, there is nothing wrong with doing a bit of retail selling for its own sake. It all represents earnings and, after all, people you might think you are simply selling to may eventually want to join the network themselves. Your prospecting will never be wasted if the least you come out of any situation with is a sale!

Do be sure that none of your prospects, just because they have signed up, think that everything is now going to happen for them. By now I should imagine you are under no illusions about the opportunity you are examining! It is not a free ride in any way and I think it is important to leave your prospects in no doubt regarding that. Tell them about the pump on the well!

As they are eventually going to have to teach others, they must be prepared to learn all they can, just as you did. I hope you feel that this book could be of real and lasting benefit to them. You need them to speak the same language as you and to pass on the same culture to the people they bring to the network. (Should you or your recruits want to obtain a copy, there is an order form at the end of the book.)

At this point, don't forget that you are not on your own. Your sponsor, if he or she is good at the job, is going to help you teach and train your famous five. Through that help and encouragement you will learn to do the same to get that all-important third level in place. There really isn't so much to learn. Apart from the MLM concept , you will also need to understand commission levels and the way in which your particular organisation is structured. You will need to learn as much about the product(s) as possible as well as the company's marketing plan.

Everything you need to know about the concept at this stage is in the book you are now holding. Do read the book through more than once. It would be a good idea, as you are reading, to use a highlighter pen to mark the statements that you regard as particularly important. This will be of great value when you are introducing others to the concept.

In a MLM organisation help is always willingly available. It is a system that somehow naturally breeds enthusiasm and an attitude of helpfulness and encouragement. The concern of everyone is their own down-line development. If your sponsor is the right sort of person, he or she will be only too willing to give you all the help you need - remember that all-important 3rd level? Well, *you* are about to produce that for him!

The effort you are going to put into your new-found enterprise will, before very long, prove to be very worthwhile.   Try not to be impatient, and don't rush things. The likelihood is that within a few months from now, you could be earning as much in a month as most people earn in four!   Doesn't that emphasise the importance of laying the right foundations and building a strong and lasting structure?

Chapter six

Let's now take a look at the time scale.

Your first month in the business is your *training month.*
Don't attempt to run too fast before you have learned to walk
properly.   There is of course nothing to stop you sponsoring
people during your training period.   Your sponsor is going to
help you all he can during this time and he will be delighted
to help you sponsor.   In training your new people he is going
to be doing most of the work whilst you receive the credit by
having names registered against your name and number.
Your business could start building almost from day one.

Your second month is *seeking and telling month.*
You will be spending most of your time seeking out your
prospects and telling them about the opportunity you are
offering them.   In the previous month you will certainly have
attended *opportunity meetings* or *business presentation
meetings.*   It is now down to you to persuade your prospects
to attend similar meetings at which the product, marketing
plan and commission structure will be professionally
explained.   As I have already said, in seeking out and
identifying your initial *serious* five, you will certainly end up
by sponsoring more than that before you find the *Gold Bricks.*

Your third month is *support month.*
This is where you begin the real work of helping and
supporting the people you have sponsored.   You are now
beginning to work towards that all-important 3rd level.   You
are teaching others how to sponsor and aiding their people in
any way you can.   The object is to dig down deeper to

establish the third and fourth levels as soon as possible. Once that is done, your support will probably not be needed to anything like the same extent, so you will have time to devote to sponsoring more people for yourself - the next row of front line 'generals' to start another down-line.

Your fourth month is income month!

At last, all the hard work and effort are beginning to pay off! The water is flowing from the pump and not so much effort is needed to keep the flow going.

It is important that throughout the initial three months you remain employed - assuming you have a full-time job - so as to maintain your income whilst working your way into this new, chosen career in your spare time. When you reach the fourth month you will probably be getting very serious because you will have the tangible evidence you need to justify all the effort. Whilst the network building is progressing, you will be moving the product constantly and earning a retail profit. Depending on your earnings, there will be a point when you should feel you could put in an even greater commitment and consider operating in MLM on a full-time basis.

During the training and establishment periods, I would urge you to attend all the opportunity, training and motivational meetings you can. Meet others doing the same as you on every possible occasion. There is a fascinating phenomenon known as *group dynamics* from which any individual can benefit greatly. Group dynamics is concerned with the energy generated by a number of people with a common cause. It can work for both good and bad, with much the same effect - *motivation.* Football hooliganism is an example of group dynamics in action in the worst possible way. The group will behave in a collective manner which is quite different to the way in which any of the individuals that constitute the group would behave on their own. Evangelical meetings, political rallies and sales conventions all use the principles of group dynamics to achieve their ends. To be part of a crowd motivated and excited by a common cause for good, can be immensely stimulating and highly beneficial to each individual's aims and ambitions.

Even small groups of people can develop their own dynamic. In MLM the effect can be to generate a great deal of enthusiasm and energy by exchanging ideas, experiences and simply striking sparks off one another. Such get togethers often occur informally after a meeting when people might have a drink at the bar. You may have brought new people to the meeting. Be sure to introduce them afterwards to as many experienced and successful people as possible over a drink, but try always to keep the conversation strictly focused on the opportunity on offer.

It is important that you are aware of the *negative attitudes* you will inevitably encounter, so that you are prepared to counter them convincingly. Always try to put people at their ease as soon as possible, if there is any element of doubt bothering them. Objections can be very counter-productive so need to be satisfactorily and professionally despatched without delay. It is most important to make sure all negatives are out of the way before you can begin to sell the ideas that really excite you. The most common and predictable objections are...

1. *Is it Pyramid Selling?*

As I have already pointed out (*page 20, & Fig 7, page 21*), the concept of the pyramid structure is fundamental to all large organisations, so must not be allowed to become a red herring! It was necessary to introduce legislation to put an end to practices that were totally unacceptable. Multi-Level/Network Marketing fully complies with that legislation, operating ethically and professionally under the watchful eye of the DTI (see *Appendix 3* at the end of the book).

2. *Won't the market soon become saturated?*

This is rather unlikely! It certainly has not been seen to happen yet. The population of the UK is approximately 60,000,000 - and that is quite a market to saturate! There are more births each year - even more houses built each year - than there are new people joining MLM organisations each year.

3. *Who buys the product?*

By now you should be able to answer that one! Many people buy it through the principle of sharing - very few *sell* it in the accepted sense.

4. *Is it like a chain letter?*

How can it be? A chain letter relies on human gullibility, superstition, even fear for its continuance. How many people have *you* met who have made a living out of a chain letter? We are talking about *real* products in MLM, not fantasies; real products with quality and value, distributed through a networking organisation designed to benefit the largest number of people without taking advantage of one of them. The customer benefits from a competitively priced product and the added value of personal service.

You will encounter all these questions. They simply represent a healthy scepticism, but it is important that you are able to answer them easily. Vague and woolly answers will merely add to the scepticism. Once the objections are out of the way, your audience will be much more willing to listen to you.

As your network begins to develop, it is vital to maintain the momentum. Remember the water pump when you stop pumping! Human beings are notorious for too easily becoming discouraged if left in isolation for very long. Make a few simple rules for yourself - and stick to them.

1. After the initial approach to a new prospect, get them along to an opportunity meeting as soon as possible.

2. Do not neglect anyone for more than a few days before introducing the next step. Depending on the particular organisation in which you are involved, this may be a more detailed opportunity meeting, a one-to-one meeting, or a training meeting. The object of any of these is to get a commitment from the interested person.

Hold your prospect's hand! Get the sponsorship form signed and arrange training as quickly as possible. Keep the interest alive and do everything to maintain the initial enthusiasm.

Do remember, everything is very strange and new, so keep in constant close contact - right up to getting the all-important third level in place. All manner of insecurities will crop up. Your new recruit will look up-line and see the success people are having, and doubts will begin to appear as to whether he or she will be capable of doing the same. They will see these people as so confident, ambitious and active, and will begin to doubt their own abilities. This is a predictable pattern so it is imperative that you are there to give your recruit confidence, to support and boost him up in every possible way. All he or she is suffering from is the natural outcome of change, in both occupation and environment.

In my own experience of sales operations, there are two important milestones on the road ahead for the new participant. The first one is *the first sale!* The second sale very often follows quickly on its heels. The next happening is often a run of sales of moderate size before the budding sales person becomes aware of the people ahead of them - those who are achieving the really big sales. They begin to worry - how could *they* ever hope to achieve such a level? But, quite suddenly, it happens! That large sale is the second important milestone, and from that day onwards confidence builds, sights are raised and horizons are broadened. What they have discovered is that *there is nothing mysterious about selling at all!* It doesn't rely on being a special type of person, but it does rely on *developing the right attitude and having a desire for success.*

In MLM your first milestone is *the day you make your first sponsorship!* The second comes after supporting that person through teaching and motivation until *they* make their first sponsorship.

The network has started
- you now know that YOU can do it!

Always demand a lot of life! Give it full measure and your rewards will be in proportion. Many people, in Britain especially, have been brought up with a vague feeling that there is something not quite decent in striving to make a lot of money! This is utter nonsense and I am happy to say, is beginning to die a death through simple economic necessity. Success and the generation of wealth can be of benefit to everyone! Enjoy making money, enjoy spending it! Spread it around, enjoy helping others to succeed, be instrumental in increasing prosperity around you in every way. Providing we have achieved our success by never taking advantage of others, by being pleased to make spontaneous gestures of help towards others without asking for either reward or recognition, we have every right to expect the very best that life can bring us.

Ask nothing of life and that is what you will get!

Success is not the result of luck! It comes from sheer hard work, commitment to an ideal, but above all from *a burning desire to succeed.*

So let's go for it! Your eventual success will have nothing to do with envying or catching up with other people. It will be the result of simply *getting started, seizing the opportunity, and not letting go until you have achieved the habit of success!*

As you set forth, doing all the right things and doing them thoroughly, think of that building of ours that will soon begin to rise, constructed on deep, secure foundations that you have created....

1 - 5 - 25...

Now things are really beginning to move and it is even more important to help and encourage all those down-line of you to dig their own foundations towards the next level...

1 - 5 - 25 - 125...

Clearly now a sizeable organisation is beginning to develop, and more importantly to you, the glittering prizes are beginning to appear as proof of everything you have been told, and as reward for all your efforts. It may have seemed slow at first - and it must be said, during this period, a lot of people lose heart - but, by this point in the development you must surely agree, it has been well worthwhile doing things properly and getting things right.

It is a matter of patient commitment -
and total dedication to your goals!

The gold prospector may spend months digging away on his claim, but he won't give up. He is spurred on constantly by his eternal optimism, sheer determination, and the belief that he *will* win in the end. How appalling it would be to give up when one more yard would uncover the seam! - but then, if he gave up, he would never know that!

1 - 5 - 25 - 125 - 625...

Chapter seven

In our prospecting how can we identify real potential, the real winners, and isolate them from the moderates, of which there are many? The *Gold Bricks* from the clay?

I have made the point at some length that MLM is not really about *selling* in the conventional sense. But, despite that, one aspect is very much about selling - and that is *prospecting*. In the context of MLM prospecting is simply *selling the opportunity* - and that can involve all the skills and subtleties of selling.

So, how are we to set about the task of seeking out and identifying our natural winners - *the Gold Bricks* - the people who will, exposed to the right degree of motivation and encouragement, become our 5 serious people? Naturally successful people are not difficult to identify since they are bristling with positive attributes. The people you are seeking will...

1...*be keen,* and anxious to learn. They will *listen* and show a willingness to *accept new ideas.*

2...ask a lot of questions and will want comprehensive answers. They will be *thinking people* and will show *natural curiosity.*

3...demonstrate a quick understanding of the opportunity and will appreciate and be excited by the multiplication.

4...show immediate commitment by *buying and using the product.*

5...know the importance of *setting goals* and will therefore achieve them without fuss.

6...be excited by the prospect of *targeting and planning*.

7...appreciate the need for active and planned prospecting. They will be willing to follow instructions and understand that, because they are being offered a system or modus operandi of proven success, there is no point in attempting to constantly reinvent the wheel.

8...be people from whom you are able to 'strike sparks'. They show a quick empathy and have great enthusiasm.

9...be *positive* people whose lives are not bounded by *if,* but by *when.*

10...have *credibility.* They will be people others will both follow and heed.

11...*will most likely be successful already!*

Now clearly, not all the people we sponsor will have all these attributes. Neither will they all turn out to be natural winners. Some will become discouraged and drop out. Be prepared for this to happen, and don't get too upset by it. All it proves is that they were probably not the right people for Network Marketing. But you should always question whether their lack of success was in any way to do with you, through, say, lack of support - or was it really that they were not suitable material?

The drop outs go to prove the value of a good and constantly growing prospect list so that you are never short of people to contact.

And now a few serious words of warning!

NEVER...

...spend time trying to rescue failures. Spend your time in developing and promoting successes! Most failures won't be saved, but naturally successful people will always respond to encouragement and recognition.

...make the mistake of telephoning your down-line and asking how many sales they have made. This goes against everything you have been teaching them. Talk about sponsoring - all you should be doing is offering help.

...show a reluctance to talk about MLM openly - and, above all, *never be mysterious about it.* This way you lose all credibility. A lack of openness merely suggests something vaguely devious. Bring all the negatives out into the open and slay the dragons right at the outset. Honesty will always reap its own reward.

...delude yourself that you can change people! Married couples spend their lives doing this *and it simply won't work!* If you start with rubbish, that is precisely what you will end up with, having wasted a great deal of time and energy to no purpose.

There is only one answer - *go for gold, and don't settle for anything less!* If you sponsor weakness, it will dilute down to rubbish in a couple of generations.

Once a person is showing the signs of failure or lack of motivation, there is nothing you can do *unless they ask for your help.* A genuine cry for help might just turn the situation around. But, if it doesn't happen quickly, let the person go for they can easily demotivate others through their negativism. Don't dissipate your energy by trying to be a lifeboat, use it for finding good replacements.

Still on the subject of basic prospecting, ask people if they have ever heard of Network Marketing or MLM. It is a useful conversational opening which gives you an easy lead into telling your story or talking about your product. Of course the product itself is a splendid starting point. Once interest has been show in it, go on to talk about the unique marketing method that is used for its distribution, and the interesting business opportunity that it presents for the right people.

To sum up this whole area of prospecting, it simply comes down to being open and honest - not creating mysteries or arousing suspicion by being devious or obtuse.

The Life Assurance industry, when it was permitted to prospect for clients, used to be amazingly good at creating its own stumbling blocks by actually encouraging its sales people to disguise their prospecting approach as much as possible when trying to get appointments. This always struck me as rather insulting to the intelligence of the prospective clients. The attitude is so negative as to contain all the seeds for its own destruction! It started with the biggest negative of all - the assumption that nobody wants to see you!

Attitude is the only answer. *But if your attitude starts from a negative assumption, you will be lead by your own beliefs into being devious, mysterious and evasive.* These are not the attitudes that should ever be associated with Network Marketing/MLM.

Be yourself and shed your inhibitions. Allow your natural excitement to come through. That way, assuming you are a reasonably intelligent person, the message will come across loud and clear! *You* are on your way to financial independence and are quite willing to show others how to achieve the same happy state for themselves! *What an exciting message!* It doesn't have to be wrapped up in contrived 'scripts' that try to put other people's words into your mouth. The result of this is often to produce a stiffness and self-consciousness that can be quite off-putting to the person on the receiving end. If you find it difficult to enthuse naturally about your product and the business opportunity you are offering, either you are not right for the job, or the product and opportunity are not right for you.

There is a little thing known as *fear of rejection,* and this is the unconscious reason that produces devious behaviour in some people. Obviously nobody likes being rejected. But rejection is a pretty strong word to use in this context. We are offering a great opportunity - it may simply be the chance to make a bit more money, or it may be the means of transforming your life. Not too many people are going to reject that! Someone may say 'no' - but that is hardly rejection. Don't let it worry you. Pass on to the next prospect.

It is fairly unlikely that, in the early stages of your involvement in Network Marketing, you will be approaching absolute strangers. Your initial prospect list will probably contain a lot of people you know in some way. If this is the case, rejection is not really an issue, is it?

You will be the best judge of what I am saying, but if you are the sort of person who can recognise the MLM opportunity and pick it up and run with it, be sure of one thing, *you will easily find the right words to pass your enthusiasm on to other people.* Enthusiasm is the most potent and infectious mode of communication!

BE POSITIVE - BE HONEST - BE YOURSELF!

Chapter eight

This chapter should really be called *'Getting to grips with Network Marketing'*.

We have examined the nuts and bolts of the concept and considered how we should tackle the business of prospecting for the people to whom we hope to offer our opportunity.

We have considered ways of making a presentation to our prospects to explain the concept in the simplest possible manner.

Let's now look at how we can keep our growing organisation on the road. Nothing will drive itself, and there is no such thing as perpetual motion. Our job, once the organisation is beginning to build, is not unlike those Chinese plate jugglers who end their act by spinning dozens of plates on long canes stuck into a rack. The juggler dashes back and forth tweaking the canes to keep the plates spinning. Inevitable, from time to time, a plate falls off and breaks...

In just the same way, from time to time in MLM someone becomes disenchanted and drops out - a broken plate. I have, throughout the book, mentioned several causes of failure - but the most common by far is lack of motivation. This could be the result of neglect and lack of contact. It could also be through lack of perceived success, almost certainly the result of impatience. You will probably realise by now that it is going to take all of three months for the rewards to begin to appear - amazingly, when you consider that they are looking at the potential of greatly enhancing their lives, many people seem unable to wait that long!

None of us works well in isolation. This is especially so in the case of MLM. We need the support and motivation that the dynamic of a group can provide. We need to know what others are doing, we need to see success, but above all, we need to tell others *what we are doing.* And we certainly need that pat on the back - *recognition!* It is that that keeps human beings motivated.

If we can recognise human weaknesses and respond to them in a positive way, we are enhancing the chances of success for everyone. All the members of a network are linked by a common bond for the growth potential has no real beginning or end. I have constantly referred to *you* and to *your* developing down-lines, but to other people *you* represent their 5th, 6th, 7th, 8th level. Everyone is inter-related and inter-dependent.

Not all your down-lines will survive by the very nature of things. One down-line may be made up of nothing but dealers or retailers wanting to make a bit of extra money. Then, quite suddenly, in that down-line, a Gold Brick appears! The person you have been waiting for, someone who sees all the potential of what is being offered and grasps it with both hands. When this happens, get to him quickly and give all the support you can. Spotting this person will only happen through good record keeping and constant down-line contact.

The Gold Brick (see *Fig.8*) is a person you should work with and encourage in every way. He or she holds the key to future development in that down-line, and can also effect your whole organisation up-line from him, simply by the example he sets. Seeing what he or she is doing could easily be instrumental in a few more Gold Bricks developing!

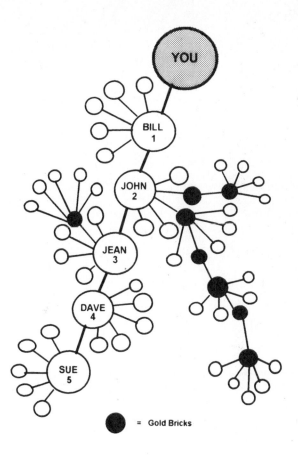

Fig. 8

So the message is, be watchful, be vigilant and keep contact at all times for you never know *when* a Gold Brick might materialise.

Contact with others should be maintained through the regular opportunity meetings and training sessions. If everyone is doing their stuff in sponsoring, the natural outcome will be that you keep meeting new people at all levels as they are brought to the various events. The key to successful development is constant group activity. Obviously it is to everyone's advantage that all types of meetings are well attended since the greatest benefit will be derived from the energy generated through numbers. It is also very desirable that the newcomers get the impression of a vital, active and dynamic organisation of which they would be pleased to be a part.

Depending on the commission structure in your particular MLM organisation, there will be a down-line cut-off point beyond which you do not earn. Some people will see this as a definite line of demarcation and will not concern themselves with expansion beyond that point. The further down the levels you work in helping and encouraging people, the better the results will be for everyone. This is just part of the collective nature of the concept. Of course you couldn't expect to have a lot of influence that far down, but that is no reason for doing nothing to help others develop the network.

The building process need never stop. You can always add to your organisation by sponsoring one or two more serious people - and *now* you can afford to be more selective - and encouraging their growth. In two to three years' time you will almost certainly be in a very healthy financial situation.

You may be wondering what happens then. Two options would probably be open to you, depending very much on the rules imposed by the particular MLM company you are attached to:

1. You could sit back and enjoy the very substantial income your endeavours would go on generating, or...

2. it may be explained to you that you have arrived at another of the fascinating spin-offs of MLM. You have developed a very considerable asset. Within some organisations, it is possible to *sell your number* to someone else, thus enabling you to retire from MLM altogether. If such a situation is available to you, it can be a very worthy target to have one's eye on.

3. The third option is obvious - to go on expanding and developing and creating greater wealth. After three or so years of really hard work, allowing one to be in the position to make these decisions, my guess would be that you would find it very difficult to give up! I have met many people in MLM who's biggest problem is finding something else to spend their money on!

Moving back a stage, many people want to know *at what stage does it make sense to become involved on a full-time basis?* The answer is **not too soon.** Use your current occupation to finance all the important outgoings such as the mortgage and the household bills whilst you are going through the learning curve. This way you will never place undue financial pressures on yourself whilst you learn this new business at the pace that suits you.

You are presumably entering this strange new world because it is of real interest to you. The time sacrifice - and that would probably only amount to about 10 hours a week initially - is a small price to pay to achieve the potential being offered. Don't allow yourself to become impatient. Prepare the foundations thoroughly and build with strength. You will know when the right time has arrived to become involved full-time, so don't even consider abandoning your regular income until your new endeavour is *at least matching it.*

We have discussed the importance of fully understanding what one must do, and the attitudes one must bring to Network Marketing if the eventual aim is real wealth creation. I have mentioned *the glittering prizes* that are dangled before the newcomer as the great incentive to become involved in MLM. I very much hope that I have persuaded you along the correct path towards your particular goal. Now perhaps, the time has come for us to take a look at what the earning potential really is.

In the normal working world there are several different types of remuneration...

1. *Direct income.*

   This derives from commissions, hourly wages etc.
   The great disadvantage of direct income is that
   if you stop work, the income ceases! This is
   what is known as *One-Dimensional-Income.*
   1 + 1 + 1 + 1 etc.

2. *Residual income.*

   This is income of an on-going nature. Good
   examples are *renewal commissions, royalties on
   books, films etc.* Developing a business which
   employs others is also residual income - the income
   continues *whether you work or not...*at least
   for a time! This is *Two-dimensional-income.*
   1 + 2 + 3 + 4 etc.

3. *Multiple income.*
This is income arising from a number of sources.
It is income of an on-going nature.
Income derived by an insurance company through
direct debit payments is a good example.
This is *Three-Dimensional-Income.*
1 + 2 + 4 + 8 + 16 + 32 + 64 etc.

Is it reasonable to assume that the man whose income is
£1,000,000 a year works 100 times harder that the man
earning £10,000?   Of course not!   In fact, the first man
could very well employ the second, and many more like him.
The millionaire has learned to work *smarter* not *harder*!   He
is very likely benefiting from the combined efforts of many
people - the multiplication of effort.

Why does a Downland hillside appear green?   Is it because
grass is green?   Yes,   of course,   but have you ever
considered what is *actually* making that hillside appear green
to your eye?
    Pick a single blade of grass and hold it up for someone to
see who is standing a hundred yards away.   Do they see it as
green?   It would be surprising if they could see it at all!   Why
then does the hillside look green when it might be a mile or
more away?   It is *the multiplication factor* - the sheer weight
of numbers.   Every single blade contributes something.   You
could prove this by removing the blades one by one;   at first,
and for some time, there would be no perceivable change, but
gradually the colour would diminish until the hillside was just
bare brown earth.

It is claimed that in the USA many millionaires have achieved
their wealth through MLM.   They have realised that the way

to make money is by utilising this multiplication process. This is not by exploiting others but, rather, by capitilizing on the efforts of many people, who are each contributing their share to the collective effort. Working *smarter* not harder.

MLM, as I pointed out in the introduction, is a system which bases its success on a very simple principle - a large number of people selling a relatively modest volume of the product. But that modest volume, exposed to the multiplication factor, becomes a vast volume of goods moved, earning startling sums of money which is spread, like the enthusiasm that generated the growth, through the system.

Everyone benefits, but the ones that benefit the most are those who recognise the necessity of putting all the ideas laid down in this book into practice.

AND IN CONCLUSION...

You are standing on the brink of a whole new life, still perhaps, a little apprehensive and uncertain.
     MLM is a growth industry of tremendous proportions.
In the United States it is said to be expanding at the rate of 30% each year, whilst in Britain, Europe and a great deal of the rest of the world, it gains an ever stronger foothold.
     You must decide whether you are *equity* driven - are you interested in building a business that will have long-term value? Or are you *income* driven - are you in MLM just for extra cash? It will take from three to five years of hard work before you have created a significant down-line. During that time you will be equity driven. Once your business is

flourishing, the investment you have made in time and effort will have created a cash machine.

Don't get discouraged! Persist and you are bound to win. Remember that *rejection* and *personnel turnover* go with the territory, they are just part of the pattern. Only between 5 and 10% of the population will be successful. Make sure you are one of them - your challenge is to find and develop some of the others!

If you approach the opportunity in a sensible, planned and committed way, and can bring to it all the right attitudes and the necessary degree of self-belief, there is no reason why you should not prosper greatly - and perhaps even become one of the millionaires that MLM has created...

My sincere hope is that through the medium of this book, I may have been instrumental in assisting you towards the greatest opportunity life has so far offered you. Make the most of it, and please, if you feel it has been worthwhile, recommend this book to others that they may benefit and prosper too!

GOOD LUCK!

Allen Carmichael - September 1995

Appendix 1

PLANNING:
Planning is of paramount importance. Without a plan and the commitment to carry it through, you will get nowhere.

If you were setting out on a journey to a place you had never visited, it would be foolish to travel without a map to tell you how far it was to your destination, and to show you the direction you should take to be sure of arriving by the shortest and most direct route. Without a map how could you know how far you had come, and how far you still had to go?

Planning is essential to achievement, and we all have fundamental needs to set both goals and targets. But simply setting goals is of little use without some sort of plan to act like a map, as a yardstick to keep us informed of both progress (or lack of it) and direction.

Setting targets and goals is a serious business and requires careful consideration if it is to have value. Goals must be precise, and the provision of a time factor is a vital ingredient to the equation. Goals must be attainable: if they are too ambitious and appear unachievable, they will have no value whatsoever - *because they are unachievable!*

So set realistic but ambitious goals with a properly mapped out route and a defined time-scale. Having done that, reduce your goal to 'bite-sized-pieces'. If you were faced with the unlikely task of eating an elephant, the only possible way to tackle the problem would be by reducing it to bite-sized-pieces. That way, given time, the task could be accomplished, unpleasant as it might be!

Reduce your eventual target then - supposing it was an earnings target for one year - firstly to a monthly figure. Next reduce that to a weekly figure, and finally, if you wish, reduce it even as far as a daily figure.   What might have looked daunting to start with, now expressed as a daily target to be achieved,   suddenly becomes both realistic and attainable.   All that is required of you now is to achieve that target day by day to be certain that the weekly, monthly and annual targets will all be realised.

Making such a plan will show clearly how you are measuring up against the time scale you have set.   It will give you a clear picture of whether you are ahead, behind, or right on target.   It is easy to see how you can beat that eventual target when you have a useful measuring tool available.

Above all, be honest with yourself.   The most stimulating way to keep a record of your progress involves one simple rule: *if you fall short* in any period *you must add the shortfall to the next period.*   But if you *exceed* your target for one period, *you disregard the excess* and accept that the target has been achieved - *you do not reduce the target for that next period!*

DON'T CHEAT YOURSELF - THAT IS THE LOSER'S WAY OF DOING THINGS

The glass half-full or the glass half-empty - the difference between optimism and pessimism...

Under targeting is a real danger since it imposes unconscious limitations on achievement.

I once took a glass jar containing some pieces of grass and a few small twigs and leaves into a sales meeting.   The top of the jar was sealed with a piece of perforated paper held in place by an elastic band. Everyone at the meeting had seen the jar in my office for several days and it had given rise to a lot of speculation.

I suggested that in the jar there were a dozen fleas, and whilst talking, I slowly removed the paper seal and gave the jar a shake. I asked what the audience thought the fleas were doing, but assured them that there was nothing to worry about since the fleas, although perfectly capable of jumping out of the jar, had conditioned themselves to the ceiling represented by the paper seal and learned to jump to a point just below that. Although they were capable of greater achievement, they had limited themselves and settled for greater comfort. They had dropped naturally into a *comfort zone* of their own devising - a most dangerous place to be!

So, in setting targets and goals, be honest and be sensibly ambitious. If things become too easy, stop the clock, establish new and more ambitious goals, and start the journey again. You must maintain your personal motivation by having goals just slightly out of reach. If targeting becomes demotivational its entire purpose is negated. If targeting is so ambitious that it appears unachievable, it becomes very dispiriting. The answer is a reassessment, a new target and a new plan.

Targeting, however, is only the first part of the plan. Having established a series of milestones so as to be able to monitor progress, the next step is to decide exactly what course of action must be followed to bring about the desired result over each step of the journey.

Your plan may revolve around your product. You may need to decide how many units of product must be moved in a given time. Or it might be to decide how many people must be contacted by telephone to fix appointments either to show the product or demonstrate your business plan with a view to sponsoring.

Every activity that is part of the plan has a value in either time, energy or cost, so prospecting distils itself down to understanding the statistical averages.

Supposing you know that each person you sponsor will provide you with immediate earnings of £200, and you also know from your records that you must contact 15 people to find one serious person to sponsor.   Then each contact is worth £13.33 - *whether you get the appointment or not!* This odd way of thinking can be a great comfort and a great motivational stimulus.   It is just a question of accepting the fact, if your statistics are accurate, of realising that you are *bound* to get a certain number of *'no'* responses before you get a *'yes'*!

A word about the importance of record keeping.   *It is of the greatest importance.*   If you come into this fascinating business, do please resolve from *day one* that you will keep accurate records of *everything* you do.   Never discard an old list of prospects - *file it!* Keep all your old diaries and notes - you never know when you may need some vital bit of information.

Keep records of all your calls, indeed, of everything you do.   Above all, keep records of every financial transaction, keep all receipts, old cheque book stubs, note down every single penny you spend in the pursuit of your business.   *Most business expenses are tax-deductible* and the time will come when you will be glad of everything you can legitimately set against taxable earnings.

One more piece of advice. Right from day one resolve to set aside at least 25% of everything you earn. Put the money into a separate account, or, better still, put it into Premium Bonds - but, put it somewhere, away from everything else.

There will be an eventual day of reckoning when the Inland Revenue demands its dues - and they don't wait, they want it *now!* You may never have been self-employed before, so do please heed this serious warning. Very many people have fallen into this particular trap - it is perhaps the commonest ailment of the self-employed - so, be prepared for it. Never say *nobody told me what to do!* Be provident, be prepared and willing to pay your way in the world, and you will never regret it. If you took up the idea of progressively putting your tax dues into Premium Bonds, who knows, you might even hit the jackpot!

Appendix 2

MOTIVATION:
We all enjoy a pat-on-the-back for a job well done. We all
need and appreciate the recognition of our peers and, perhaps
even more importantly, the recognition our superior may
publicly bestow on us.

For someone like you who is going to depend on quality
and the ability of others to sponsor and teach in the way you
have shown them, it is so important that you understand the
significance of *recognition* as a factor in the development of
your business. It is perhaps the most valuable tool you posses
to aid and promote the growth of your down-lines. Make this
part of your teaching, for it cannot be emphasised too
strongly.

Happiness, satisfaction, self-image and motivation all owe
their being to recognition. In industry generally, the greatest
single mistake that is made by management is to assume that,
because an individual is doing well and demonstrating the
signs of reasonable success, he no longer has a need for
recognition. It is the greatest fallacy to believe that as
success increases, the need for recognition diminishes.

The successful person is still a human being with all the
frailties and insecurities that go with the territory. And the
greatest of these needs is the need for recognition.

In the development of down-lines in Network Marketing,
recognition for progress and effort will pay the highest
dividends. As a leader, assuming that is how you would like
to think of yourself, maintaining personal contact,
demonstrating commitment to others and an appreciation of

the importance of fundamental human needs, are the skills you must master.

As with all situations involving large numbers of people, *retention* is a perpetual problem. If you can get everyone to seriously follow all the basic principles I have laid out in this book, retention should not be a significant worry. I am often asked what is the single most significant factor in MLM success. The answer is simple. Keep your eye on your goal, and do not allow yourself to be distracted *by any other newly launched, green-field opportunity* for *at least three months.* And the second most important factor is *to teach the people you sponsor to do the same!* This way, retention will never be a real problem and growth and development will be guaranteed.

Once you have sponsored a person, it is more important to help that person to sponsor others than to concentrate on your own sponsorship. The importance should always be placed on *building in depth rather than width.* Remember, the aim is to *replicate yourself* by digging down to that third level as soon as possible. If you make it a rule to help your front line to help *their* front line to maintain the quality, the Gold Bricks *will* begin to appear, and, with your finger always on the pulse, you will certainly spot them, *for they are the trigger to faster and better development.*

Set the right example, maintain the ethical standards and the quality of your sponsorship to ensure that only the best materials are being used, and yours will be a fine, strong building that nothing can rock. And, to keep it strong and to keep it developing, *remember always to recognise achievement.*

Appendix 3

A FEW NOTES ON THE LEGISLATION:
In the United Kingdom (and of course, in other countries, the legislation could be different) there are two *'Statutory Instruments'* with which all MLM or Network Marketing schemes must comply.   They are:
>*The Pyramid Selling Schemes Regulations 1989 (No2195).*
>*The Pyramid Selling Schemes (Amendment) Regulations 1990 (No.150).*

Copies of both the above may be obtained from:
 H.M.Stationery Office, PO Box No.276, London. SW8 5DT
Telephone: 0171 873 9090.

The Department of Trade and Industry (DTI) has produced an excellent pamphlet which adequately sums up the main points of Government legislation.   The title of this is
'Multi-Level Selling Schemes. A guide to the
Pyramid Selling Schemes Legislation.'

The rules governing Pyramid,   Multi-Level   or Networking selling deal with the following four points:
The information with which people should be provided
when being invited to join a scheme.
The rights of the participants.
The content of contracts.
Illegal payments.

The DTI pamphlet is very fair in its assessments and points out that hard work is essential to success.   It gives sound advice by emphasising the need for confidence in the product and its realistic pricing.   Further, it advises that you ensure that the difference between your own buying and selling prices leaves a sufficient margin to provide a realistic income.

In choosing a plan, make sure you have been provided with sufficient written information explaining the plan. Choose one which concentrates on *both* selling *and* recruiting others. Be sure that you believe in the product or service you are promoting and check that there is a demand for such goods or services in your area. Other things to be sure of are that the company provides proper and adequate training (although in some cases there may be a charge for this), and that you receive a written contract stating your rights and giving the equally required *statutory warning*.

Copies of the DTI pamphlet may be obtained from:

The Department of Trade and Industry,
Consumer Affairs Division 3, 10-18 Victoria Street,
LONDON SW1H 0NN
Telephone: 0171 215 3344

(This is an answering service for the ordering of leaflets) Common sense dictates the safeguards by which you should sensibly abide. Don't...part with any money without reading the small print in any document or contract. Don't outlay money on products unless you are sure you can dispose of those products. You must feel total confidence in:

the organisation you will be a part of,
the individuals with whom you will be working,
the product or service you will be selling,
...but, most of all - YOURSELF!

Author's note: It is a fact that Pyramid Selling is not illegal - it is simply that certain aspects of it have been controlled by legislation. It is a pity, in view of the fact that the term Pyramid Selling has become synonymous in most minds with unethical practices, that the DTI booklet still uses it.

Appendix 4

RECORD KEEPING:

Throughout the book there have been mentions of the importance of record keeping. To aid you in your recruitment and sponsoring, the following pages contain copies of a simple diagrammatic form that should be of use to you.

The boxes numbered 1 to 5 are for the insertion of the names of your *serious* 5 - your front-line generals, the people who show all the signs of enthusiasm and understanding to begin a down-line development of their own.

Below the diagram are spaces to record the people we referred to as *dealers* or *retailers* - the people who are joining you because they simply want to make a bit of extra income to supplement their employed income.

The five further pages are to record the progress of your initial five, with spaces for *their* serious 5. On each of those pages, the name of one of your initial 5 goes into the top panel. There is also space to record *their* dealers or retailers. The diagrams then, represent a complete record of the first 30 people in *your* down-lines (as well as the dealers and retailers), and should be invaluable for maintaining constant contact for, everything that happens from that point on *is that all-important 3rd level.*

If you are involved in an organisation, for example, that prefers sponsoring in *sixes*, you could easily adapt the diagrammatic forms for yourself on paper. These could then be photocopied for use within your down-line.

Appendix 5

A NOTE ON THE USE OF THIS BOOK:
From the feed-back *CONCEPT* has received, it is clear that
this book has enjoyed particular success when utilised in one
or two specific ways.   It is known to have brought literally
thousands of people into the Network Marketing business,
firstly because of what has been described as its clarity and its
brevity, and secondly because it can be read in a matter of an
hour or two. This, we are told, is what people new to the
concept of Network Marketing need - a quick and accurate
idea of what-it-is-all-about!

Many people attend meetings staged by Distributors with
successful down-line developments working for a multitude of
companies.   These may be described as Opportunity
Meetings,   Business or Marketing Plan Presentations etc.
Whatever they are called,   they have one common
denominator - they are designed to *sell* the idea of Network
Marketing (MLM) to the newcomer, and particularly to sell it
linked to the specific product(s) or service of one company.
   Since any such meeting will include a high proportion of
people entirely new to Network Marketing, a certain amount
of scepticism is bound to exist amongst the members of the
audience - scepticism of the *well-you-would-say-that-wouldn't
-you!* variety.   If, at the end of such a meeting,   the
newcomers are introduced to this little book - either being
given it, sold it, or lent it - to take away and read at home, the
results have been shown to be most interesting.
   Any opportunity meeting will have a 'drift-away' factor
of around 50% - people who have not been convinced or still

remain sceptical. We know from many users of this book, that the 50% drift-away factor can be turned around and become very nearly a 100% take-up. We have questioned many people as to how this happens and the general opinion seems to be that the people who take the book away with them get another description and another view of the concept of Network Marketing - *probably exactly the same information as they heard at the meeting, **but from a completely independent source.*** And it is *that* that gives the presentation they attended much greater credibility.

Allen Carmichael has always believed that it is important to understand the concept of Network Marketing even before being introduced to a company's product(s). This book has been known to excite people about the *idea,* even before they have met anyone involved in the business. The book has been successfully used as a prospecting tool, sent out, given or lent, to people with a note saying the sender will be in contact in a day or two to see what the recipient's reaction is. This does not have to be as costly as it sounds since the book can always be retrieved from anyone who turns out not to be interested. The great point that has been learned is that the time anyone is given to read the book should be little more than 48 hours. Human nature being what it is, the longer the string paid out, the less likely the action!

Finally, the Allen Carmichael books are available in English in Australia, New Zealand, Hong Kong, China, Korea, Thailand, The Philippines, Taiwan, Malasia, Indonesia, Brunei, Taiwan, South Africa, Namabia, Botswana, Zimbabwe, Lesotho & Swaziland. There is now also a Finnish translation of the first book. This information may be useful to Distributors who have developed down-lines overseas.

For fully up-to-date information please contact us...
CONCEPT - **Phone/Fax: 01323 485434**

FIRST LEVEL DEVELOPMENT

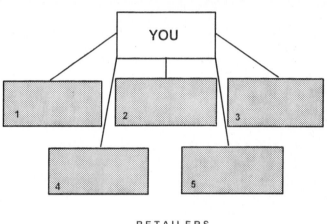

RETAILERS

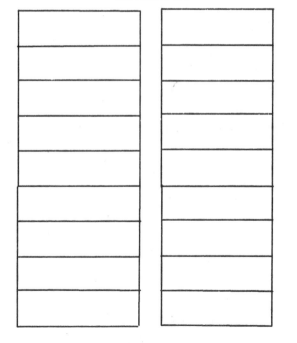

NOTES

SECOND LEVEL DEVELOPMENT

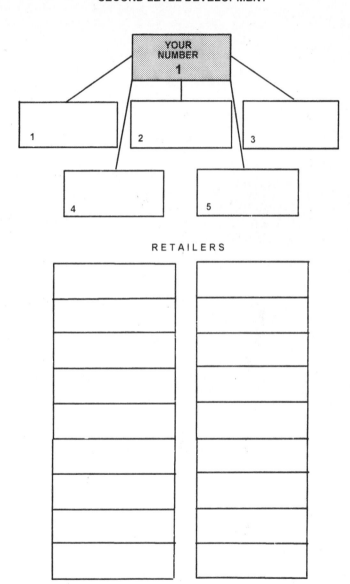

RETAILERS

NOTES

SECOND LEVEL DEVELOPMENT

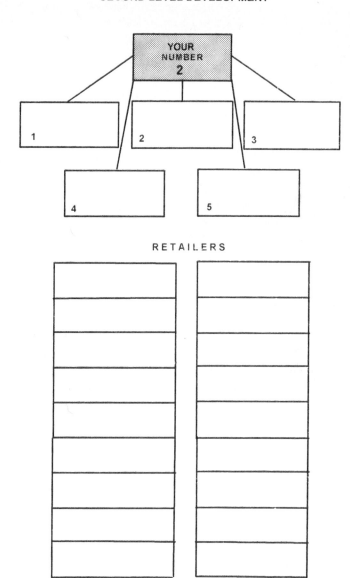

RETAILERS

NOTES

SECOND LEVEL DEVELOPMENT

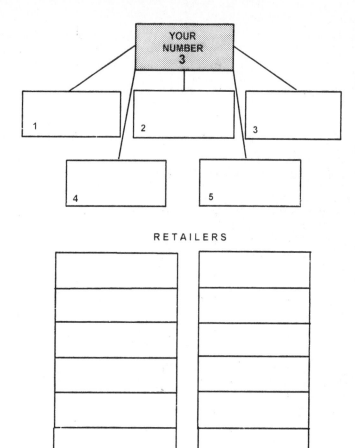

YOUR NUMBER 3

1

2

3

4

5

RETAILERS

NOTES

SECOND LEVEL DEVELOPMENT

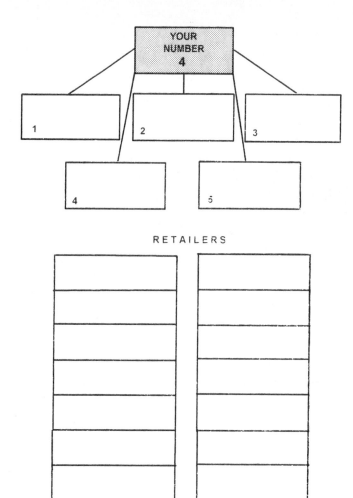

RETAILERS

NOTES

SECOND LEVEL DEVELOPMENT

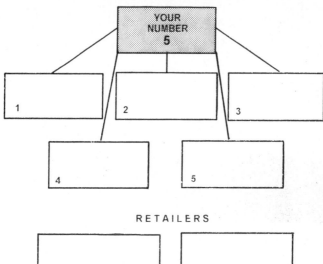

RETAILERS

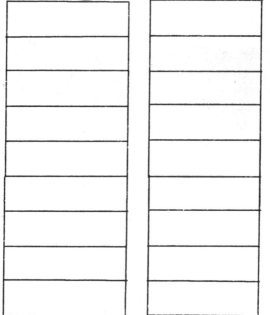

The Network Marketing
Self-Starter *(2nd edition)*

By Allen Carmichael

The name Allen Carmichael has become synonymous with Network Marketing. This, his second book on the subject, was written in response to demands for more information from people who had become fascinated by the Network Marketing/MLM concept, after reading his introductory book, *'Network & Multi-Level Marketing'*.

Network Marketing is a business concept requiring, for the success it can bring, a high degree of motivation and commitment from its devotees. The 'Network Marketing Self-Starter' takes, as its starting point, all the aspects covered in Allen Carmichael's first book, and expands them into a training course. The book is packed with useful and practical information.

It includes *The 100 days plan*, described by many as the ultimate guide to networking achievement. The plan is designed to provide, for those prepared to commit themselves completely to its simple formula, all the evidence the reader will ever need to convince him or her that high earnings are not just possible, *they are realistically achievable* - to people who are dedicated to the idea of *achieving the habit of success*...and the book includes a chapter on exactly that.

£7.50

Please see the order form at the end of this book

CONCEPT

Believe you can!

By Allen Carmichael

This is a book for anyone who wants to change their life!
It is based on the simple fact that *anyone can achieve anything* providing they believe strongly enough in the possibility.

It is never too late to change or to make adjustments to the personality.   The book explains in the first place why we are what we are and then leads the reader through a series of exercises designed to uncover personal potential.   This information is then used as the basis for an Action Plan that will ensure success and achievement in what ever area of change or adjustment the reader is concentrating on.

The feed-back the publishers have had endorses the book's strength. It has certainly changed lives!   It has been instrumental in giving new hope to people injured by the general world economic situation - people made redundant,   people who have lost money,   jobs, businesses. In short, people who feel they have been short-changed by life, but are prepared to do something positive about getting back their self-esteem and enjoying really living once again.

Failure in life is not just falling down, but rather, having fallen down, not having the wit, guts or determination to get up and start again...

This is the book for anyone with a real desire to become a success

£6.99

Please see the order form at the end of this book

CONCEPT

Four-Square-Selling
By Allen Carmichael

Every one of us is involved in selling!
In putting across any idea, whether we are seeking to influence others or just persuading them to our way of thinking, *we are selling!*

Marriage is the ultimate example of successful sales technique, and the maintenance of on-going relationships is dependant on the *buying* and *selling* of ideas and attitudes. The same techniques we employ in successful living, work in precisely the same way in the sale of goods and services - and *that,* basically, is what *Four-Square-Selling* is all about. It is concerned very much with people, and especially with the difference between excellence and mediocrity.

Any company with goods or services to market needs men and women to sell them - people who not only act as the stimulators of profit and expansion, but are also ambassadors for the organisations that employ them.

The book contains a wealth of information beyond the *Four-Square-Selling* system itself. There is a section on the identification of personal *style* and how best to treat people of differing personality. There is a fool-proof record keeping system and a working plan designed to maximise on success whilst only working a *four-day-week.*

The theme that runs through all Allen Carmichael's books is that of the pursuit of excellence, motivated by the right ethical and practical ideas. He writes of the psychology of success in a down-to-earth manner that has helped many thousands of people to bring both change and excitement to their lives.

£7.99

Please see the order form at the end of this book

CONCEPT

ORDER & REGISTRATION FORM (NMLM3)

Please supply........................copies
NETWORK & MULTI-LEVEL MARKETING - 3rd Ed. (ISBN 1 873288 14 X) **£4.99**

Please supply ....copies
THE NETWORK MARKETING SELF-STARTER - 2nd Ed.(ISBN 1 873288 09 3)
£7.50

Please supply ....copies
BELIEVE YOU CAN! (ISBN 1 873288 03 4) **£6.99**

Please supply ....copies
FOUR-SQUARE-SELLING (ISBN 1 873288 04 2) **£7.99**

**U.K. (only)Postage & Packing charges: 1 book = .50p 2 books = .85p
3 books = £1.35 4 books = £1.75**

Cheque/P.O for the sum of....................enclosed, including P&P charge
Please make cheques and postal orders payable to CONCEPT
Discount prices for bulk orders are available on request

TITLE (Mr. Mrs. Miss. Ms)..

FIRST NAMES..

SURNAME...

ADDRESS..

....

POST CODE......................PHONE/FAX.........................../.........................

It would be of interest to us if you would answer the following questions:
Where did you buy this book?..
Are you in Network Marketing?......Which Network?...............................

CONCEPT Publishers and Distributors of the Allen Carmichael books

P.O.Box 614 . P O L E G A T E . East Sussex . B N 26 5 S S . England
Telephone & Fax: 01323 485434

From experience we know that once a reader has
used the Order Form in this book,
they have no record of our address and telephone number!

So that the book still contains a permanent record,
the information is as follows...

CONCEPT
Publishers & Distributors of the Allen Carmichael books

P.O.Box 614.   POLEGATE .   East Sussex . BN26 5SS   . England

Telephone/Fax: 01323 485434

PROSPECTING LIST

From school days - College/University/Tech. - Church/Club/Society - Employment/occupation - Who
do I buy from? - Who delivers to me? - Parents of children's friends - Neighbours - Social friends -
Met on holidays - etc.

NAME	ADDRESS	PHONE	DATE

PROSPECTING LIST

From school days - College/University/Tech. - Church/Club/Society - Employment/occupation - Who do I buy from? - Who delivers to me? - Parents of children's friends - Neighbours - Social friends - Met on holidays - etc.

NAME	ADDRESS	PHONE	DATE

PROSPECTING LIST

From school days - College/University/Tech. - Church/Club/Society - Employment/occupation - Who do I buy from? - Who delivers to me? - Parents of children's friends - Neighbours - Social friends - Met on holidays - etc.

NAME	ADDRESS	PHONE	DATE

PROSPECTING LIST

From school days - College/University/Tech. - Church/Club/Society - Employment/occupation - Who do I buy from? - Who delivers to me? - Parents of children's friends - Neighbours - Social friends - Met on holidays - etc.

NAME	ADDRESS	PHONE	DATE